The Pipe Smoker

200 Trivia Questions for Pipe Smokers

Compiled by Hugh Morrison

Montpelier Publishing
London
2016

ISBN-13: 978-1535180825
ISBN-10: 153518082X

Published by Montpelier Publishing, London.

Printed by Amazon Createspace.

This edition copyright © 2016. All rights reserved.

Quiz 1

1. What is the only James Bond film in which Bond smokes a pipe?

2. Which tobacco shows a judge on the tin?

3. Who invented the Falcon pipe?

4. What are Drikule basket filters made of?

5. What is the difference between a Rhodesian and a Bulldog pipe?

6. What significant event for pipe smokers occurred in the United Kingdom on 1 July 2007?

7. Which British pipe smoking Member of Parliament died on 14 March 2014?

8. What is the name of the black rubber traditionally used to make pipe mouthpieces?

9. For many years, French tobacconist shops displayed a picture of two men, one smoking a pipe and the other smoking a cigarette. What was the slogan used with the picture?

10. Dr Perl charcoal filters have a white tip and a blue tip. Which tip should face the bowl?

Quiz 2

Complete the following advertising slogans for pipe tobacco:

1. Join the _____.

2. Nothing should disturb that_____ moment.

3. PA means Pipe Appeal, means _____.

4. Edgeworth smokes_____.

5. Live in peace with your pipe with _____.

6. St Bruno: the _____ of pipe smokers.

7. Gold Block: _____and smoke it.

8. Captain Black: _____in a bowl.

9. Dr Grabow: the world's only _____pipes.

10. Granger: right for_____.

Quiz 3

1. What is the Frank Method used for?

2. Who wrote *The Pipe Book*?

3. Who said 'The pipe draws wisdom from the lips of the philosopher, and shuts up the mouth of the foolish'?

4. What was said to be Hugh Hefner's favourite tobacco?

5. A 'Missouri Meerschaum' pipe is more commonly known as what?

6. Which tobacco was created by Benjamin Hartwell to impress ladies while out walking?

7. What pipe shop, now defunct, was housed in one of the only 16th century buildings in London?

8. What type of tobacco is named after a city in Syria?

9. What pipe shape shares its name with a Scottish peerage?

10. What pipe factory was located at Brentford, Middlesex, England?

Quiz 4

1. What material are Philtpad filters made from?

2. What is usually said to the minimum number of pipes one should have in a rotation?

3. Who had a 'three pipe problem'?

4. A new pipe brand was created when Falcon pipes removed two letters from their company name due to a trademark dispute. What was the new name?

5. Which pipe maker, established in 1876, is based in Milan, Italy?

6. Which sports car designer also produces pipes?

7. Who was the last British prime minister to smoke a pipe?

8. What pipe shape is named after an office in the Church of England?

9. What tobacconist and pipe seller is based on the island of Guernsey in the Channel Islands?

10. What is the literal English translation of 'meerschaum'?

Quiz 5

1. Which pipe tobacco was advertised with a St Bernard dog?

2. Which American writer said 'if I cannot smoke in heaven I will not go'?

3. Which pipe maker created the 'P-Lip' system?

4. In which French town were the first briar pipes made?

5. What is the latin name for tobacco?

6. Which king wrote *A Counterblaste to Tobacco*?

7. Which company manufactures 'magic inch' pipes?

8. Who was the last president of the USA to smoke a pipe while in office?

9. Which Dunhill tobacco is named after part of a child's anatomy?

10. Which tobacco manufacturer has the highest number of reviews at tobaccoreviews.com?

Quiz 6

1. What is the name of the substance smoked by the Hobbits in *The Lord of the Rings*?

2. Which tobacco is named after something found at the bottom of an American river?

3. Which tobacco was blended for the Moderator of the Church of Scotland and later became a favourite of British Prime Minister Stanley, Earl Baldwin?

4. In what type of pipe would you find a 'dry ring'?

5. Which pipe maker uses a balsa wood filter system?

6. What is the name given to the soggy bits of tobacco left at the bottom of a bowl?

7. Why is it inadvisable to use a piece of apple to hydrate tobacco?

8. Which British boxer was awarded 'Pipe Smoker of the Year' in 1984?

9. Which tobacco is named after an English explorer of the sixteenth century?

10. Who said 'I believe pipe smoking contributes to a somewhat calm and objective judgement in all human affairs'?

Quiz 7

1. Whose pipes feature a small white dot on the stem?

2. What is the name of the rough finish on a briar bowl?

3. Which company manufactures 'Dinky Bent' pipes?

4. What type of cut is used in Clan tobacco?

5. Which flake tobacco, made by Player's, is also slang for an Australian soldier?

6. What nationality is pipe maker Eric Nording?

7. What type of tobacco was first grown on a large scale on the farm of Captain Frederick Kautz in Ohio in 1864?

8. What are the four main types of tobacco curing?

9. Baseball player Billy Martin advertised what tobacco in the 1980s?

10. Which Dunhill tobacco tin shows a picture of a cockerel?

Quiz 8

1. What is the generic name for pipes that do not conform to a standard shape?

2. What feature usually distinguishes a pipe lighter from a cigarette lighter?

3. What tobacco was named after the husband of an English queen?

4. In what month does International Pipe Smoking Day usually take place?

5. What is the number one selling pipe tobacco in the USA?

6. What brand of tobacco is named after the former currency of Portugal?

7. What type of tobacco is usually the major component of an English blend?

8. What type of tobacco comes from St James Parish, Louisiana, USA?

9. Rope tobacco is also known as what?

10. Which English essayist said 'May my last breath be drawn through a pipe, and exhaled in a jest'?

Quiz 9

1. What tobacco is named after both a drink and an item of clothing?

2. What type of tobacco shares its name with the family name of the Duke of Devonshire?

3. Izmir, Samsun and Yenidji are all types of what tobacco?

4. What is the defining feature of shag cut tobacco?

5. Which company manufactures 'Sunset Breeze' tobacco?

6. What pipe company was set up in the 1920s specifically to market Dunhill 'seconds'?

7. Which brand of pipe tobacco shows a World War One biplane on the tin?

8. The 'Wunup' pipe of the 1930s was made from which man-made material?

9. Sherlock Holmes is most commonly depicted smoking which type of pipe?

10. What pipe shape, named after a type of horseman, has a shank which extends beyond the bowl?

Quiz 10

1. What was the principal ingredient in the children's sweet known as 'pipe tobacco'?

2. What tobacco is named after an island in the East Frisians?

3. Who painted a picture of a pipe entitled 'This is not a pipe'?

4. Which brand of 1970s aftershave, made by Avon, came in a pipe shaped bottle?

5. Which French company, later based in London, was the first to mass-market briar pipes?

6. What is a 'stinger'?

7. What pipe shape is named after an African tribe?

8. The bowl and shank of a pipe are collectively known as what?

9. The type of wood known as 'bog oak' used to make pipes is also known by what other name?

10. What do General Douglas MacArthur and Popeye the Sailor have in common?

Quiz 11

1. The material known as 'brylon' used for making pipes is composed of what?

2. Why is a 'block meerschaum' pipe more expensive than ordinary meerschaum?

3. Captain Pete, Erica and Kinsale are all pipe companies selling seconds from which manufacturer?

4. Big Ben and Croydon pipes are made in which country?

5. In pipe tobacco manufacture what is meant by the term 'casing'?

6. What tobacco is named after a senior rank in the British Army which is not a rank of the US Army?

7. What is the term for a residual tobacco taste in a pipe?

8. What is an ebauchon block?

9. What is the name given to a pipe with a stem which fits into a metal casing within the shank?

10. What is a 'softie'?

Quiz 12

1. What is the name for a small flat-bowled pipe with a rotating stem?

2. What pipe smoker's accessory is named after a European country?

3. What is the name given to a sealed jar for tobacco?

4. What is another name for a simple tamper?

5. What is 'faux pipe tobacco' in the USA made from?

6. Who wrote *In Defense of Smokers*?

7. What is a basket pipe?

8. What is another term for a second hand pipe?

9. What is a 'pinch test' used for?

10. What is the technical term for a pipe which comes with a ready-made cake?

Quiz 13

1. What is the name given to the first light of a pipe?

2. Which tobacconist is located at 19, St James' Street, London, England?

3. Which company makes tobaccos named after English seaside resorts?

4. Which tobacco comes in a tin which shows a picture of Paul Revere?

5. Which aromatic tobacco shares its name with an American jazz record label?

6. What pipe shape shares its name with a card game?

7. What pipe shape is named after an African country which changed its name in 1980?

8. How does a Falcon International pipe differ from a Falcon pipe?

9. Amber was once used for pipe stems. What is it made from?

10. What is the term used to describe sugar crystallisation on tobacco?

Quiz 14

1. What is the English name for *erica arborea*?

2. What is the name for the raised part of a pipe's mouthpiece?

3. What is the technical term for the smell or aroma of a tobacco indoors?

4. What is unusual about a 'Zeppelin' pipe?

5. A Squat Rhodesian shape is also known as what?

6. What is the name for a piece of tobacco cut from a rope or twist?

7. What was the purpose of the small spur on the underside of clay pipes?

8. Who wrote *Pipe Smoking: a 21st Century Guide*?

9. Which tobacco is named after a Florida town which was the setting for a 1948 film starring Humphrey Bogart and Lauren Bacall?

10. What area of south-east Europe gives its name to a type of tobacco?

Quiz 15

1. Which tobacco manufacturer was the last to hold the Royal Warrant of HM Queen Elizabeth II?

2. What unusual material were Venturi pipes made from?

3. A pipe can be smoked upside-down. True or false?

4. What tobacco is named after a village in *The Lord of the Rings*?

5. Which trade body represents tobacconists in the City of London?

6. In which country are Mattner, Jobert, and Goussard pipes made?

7. After being sued by Dunhill for copying its white stem dot, which company thereafter manufactured pipes with four white stem dots in a diamond pattern?

8. Which French pipe brand name was created by the union of two company names, Comoy and Chapuis?

9. Which pipes with a medical sounding name were originally made in France but are now made in Britain?

10. Which tobacco company name relates to the American Declaration of Independence?

Quiz 16

1. Umbria, Lombardo and Como tobaccos are produced by which company?

2. Who produces Fourth Generation tobacco?

3. Which iconic French cigarette brand also produces a pipe tobacco of the same name?

4. On which small Mediterranean island are Comino and Grand Master pipes manufactured?

5. What is the name of the Swedish pipe similar in design to the Falcon?

6. Who was the last person to receive the title 'Pipe Smoker of the Year' before the awards ceased in 2003?

7. Which pipe smoking organisation produces the magazine *Rokringar*?

8. Which American tobacconist shop chain produces Sherlock's Choice tobacco?

9. Which pipe brand's logo features the letter 'S' topped with a crown?

10. Hungarian cobbler Karol Kovacs is said to have been the first maker of what?

Quiz 17

1. Which famous children's writer also wrote a book on pipe smoking entitled *My Lady Nicotine*?

2. What is the name of the quarterly magazine dedicated to pipe smoking which was published between 1964 and 2005?

3. Which famous painter produced a number of pipe smoking self-portraits?

4. What tobacco, produced by Thomas Radford, is named after a day of the week?

5. Which famous British tobacconist produced Capstan and Three Castles tobacco?

6. Which tobacco company is named after a region of southern England made famous by the author Thomas Hardy?

7. What is 'birdseye'?

8. What is another name for an acrylic stem, particularly a patterned one?

9. Which Dunhill tobacco attempts to replicate the first type of tobacco smoked in England?

10. What tobacco was smoked both by left-wing politician Tony Benn and right-wing TV character Alf Garnett?

Quiz 18

1. Which writer appeared in an advertisement for Player's Navy Cut pipe tobacco in 1909?

2. Which pipe uses the 'drinkless' system?

3. The Carey Magic Inch cooling system works on the same principle as which part of a car's engine?

4. The design of the Falcon pipe system is said to have been inspired by what meteorological phenomenon?

5. What brand of bowl filter is made from processed silica?

6. What company makes 'keystone' filters?

7. What type of pipe did outdoor bowls champion David Bryant usually smoke?

8. Which traditional English tobacconist has branches in Bath and Oxford?

9. True or false: a British soldier in uniform may only smoke a pipe if he removes his head-covering first.

10. Which tobacco comes in a tin with a picture of a waiter holding a tray of drinks?

Quiz 19

1. What is the name of the company owned by pipe maker Mark Tinsky?

2. Which pipe maker's logo shows the letter 'S' on a shield topped with two pipes?

3. What three-letter British pipe name merged with Comoy in 1981?

4. What brand of pipe is named after a pipe-smoking American physician who died in 1965 at the age of 97?

5. Which company produces tobaccos named after places in the English Lake District?

6. What term is used to describe American tobaccos which are readily available in most shops?

7. Which American city is known as 'The corn cob capital of the world'?

8. Which famous pipe smoker had a bucket of water thrown over him by his servant?

9. Which 1930s Hollywood actor, famous for playing gangsters, has a tobacco named after him?

10. What is propylene glycol used for in tobacco manufacture?

Quiz 20

1. What American tobacco comes in a tin with a white dog on a blue background?

2. Sherlock Holmes' companion Dr Watson also smoked a pipe. True or false?

3. Which fictional pipe-smoking detective only smoked cigarettes when portrayed on screen by Humphrey Bogart?

4. What term is used to describe the carbonised deposits on the inside of a pipe bowl?

5. What is the name of the top part of a piece of briar when used in pipe making?

6. What is the essential characteristic of a 'windshield' pipe?

7. Who is thought to have made the first sandblasted pipe?

8. What country does drama tobacco usually come from?

9. What tobacco type takes its name from an English queen?

10. What was the most commonly used pipe-making material before briar?

Answers

Quiz 1

1. *On Her Majesty's Secret Service.*
2. Orlik Golden Sliced.
3. Kenly Bugg.
4. Wire.
5. A Rhodesian has a round shank, a Bulldog has a diamond shaped shank.
6. Smoking was banned indoors in public places.
7. Tony Benn.
8. Vulcanite.
9. *La Pipe Est Mieux* (The Pipe Is Better).
10. The white tip.

Quiz 2

1. Clan.
2. Condor.
3. Prince Albert.
4. Coolest.
5. Mellow Virginia Flake from Benson and Hedges.
6. Patron saint.
7. Put that in your pipe.
8. Never a bite.
9. Pre-smoked.
10. Your pipe.

Quiz 3

1. Packing a pipe.
2. Alfred Dunhill.
3. William Makepeace Thackeray.
4. Sutliff's Mixture No. 79.
5. A corncob.
6. 'Evening Stroll'.
7. Shervington's of Holborn.
8. Latakia.
9. Lovat.
10. Falcon.

Quiz 4

1. Chalk.
2. 3.
3. Sherlock Holmes
4. Alco.
5. Savinelli.
6. Porsche.
7. Harold Wilson.
8. Churchwarden.
9. EA Carey.
10. Sea foam.

Quiz 5

1. St. Bruno.
2. Mark Twain.
3. Peterson.
4. St Claude.
5. *Nicotiana tabacum*.
6. James I of England and VI of Scotland.
7. E A Carey.
8. Gerald Ford.
9. Baby's Bottom.
10. McLelland.

Quiz 6

1. 'Pipe-Weed'.
2. Mississipi Mud
3. Presbyterian Mixture
4. A Falcon.
5. Savinelli.
6. Dottle.
7. It can cause mould growth.
8. Sir Henry Cooper.
9. Sir Walter Raleigh.
10. Albert Einstein.

Quiz 7

1. Dunhill.
2. Rustic.
3. Dr Plumb.
4. Ribbon Cut.
5. Digger.
6. Danish.
7. Burley
8. Fire, air, sun, flue.
9. Captain Black.
10. Early Morning Pipe.

Quiz 8

1. Freehand.
2. The flame comes from the side.
3. Prince Albert.
4. February.
5. Captain Black.
6. Escudo.
7. Latakia.
8. Perique.
9. Twist.
10. Charles Lamb.

Quiz 9

1. Nightcap.
2. Cavendish.
3. Oriental.
4. It is very finely shredded.
5. Peterson.
6. Parker.
7. Squadron Leader.
8. Bakelite.
9. Gourd Calabash.
10. Cavalier.

Quiz 10

1. Shredded coconut.
2. Borkum Riff.
3. René Magritte.
4. Thai Winds.
5. Comoy.
6. A metal stem filter.
7. Zulu.
8. Stummel.
9. Morta.
10. They both smoked corncob pipes.

Quiz 11

1. Resin and sawdust.
2. It is made from one single piece rather than a composite.
3. Peterson.
4. The Netherlands.
5. Flavouring.
6. Brigadier.
7. Ghost.
8. A block of briar before it is turned into a machine made pipe.
9. Army or military mount.
10. A rubber cover for a pipe bit.

Quiz 12

1. Vest Pocket Pipe.
2. Czech pipe tool.
3. Humidor.
4. Pipe nail.
5. Cigarette tobacco, to avoid tax.
6. Lauren A Colby.
7. A cheap pipe, often a second or unbranded.
8. Estate pipe.
9. To determine moisture level in tobacco.
10. Pre-carbonized.

Quiz 13

1. Charring light or false light.
2. James J Fox.
3. Esoterica Tobacciana.
4. Midnight Ride.
5. Blue Note.
6. Poker.
7. Rhodesian.
8. One has a black stem, the other is bare metal.
9. Fossilised tree resin.
10. Bloom.

Quiz 14

1. Briar.
2. Button.
3. Room note.
4. It has a sealed horizontal bowl.
5. Bullmoose.
6. Coin.
7. To enable it to be stood upright on a table.
8. Richard Carleton Hacker.
9. Key Largo.
10. The Balkans.

Quiz 15

1. Gallaher.
2. Plastic and pyrolitic graphite.
3. True.
4. Frog Morton.
5. The Worshipful Company of Tobacco Pipe Makers and Tobacco Blenders.
6. South Africa.
7. Sasieni.
8. Chacom.
9. Dr Plumb.
10. 1776 Tobacco Company.

Quiz 16

1. Caminetto.
2. Erik Stokkebye.
3. Gauloises.
4. Malta.
5. Brilon.
6. Stephen Fry.
7. The Pipe Club of Sweden.
8. Tinder Box.
9. Stanwell.
10. A meerschaum pipe.

Quiz 17

1. JM Barrie.
2. The Pipe Smoker's Ephemeris.
3. Van Gogh.
4. Sunday's Fantasy.
5. WD and HO Wills.
6. Wessex.
7. A bowl grain pattern.
8. Lucite.
9. Elizabethan Mixture.
10. St. Bruno.

Quiz 18

11. Mark Twain.
12. Kaywoodie.
13. Carburettor.
14. Rainfall.
15. Denicool Crystals.
16. Nording.
17. Falcon Bent.
18. Frederick Tranter.
19. True.
20. Dunhill Aperitif.

Quiz 19

1. The American Pipe Smoking Co.
2. Savinelli.
3. GBD.
4. Dr Grabow.
5. Samuel Gawith.
6. Drug store blends.
7. Washington, Missouri.
8. Sir Walter Raleigh.
9. Edward G. Robinson.
10. As a humectant (moisturing agent).

Quiz 20

1. Granger.
2. True.
3. Philip Marlowe.
4. Cake.
5. Plateaux.
6. The bowl is higher in the front than the back.
7. Alfred Dunhill.
8. Greece.
9. Virginia.
10. Clay.

Other pipe books from Montpelier Publishing

The Pipe Smoker's Companion

An anthology of the best poetry and prose from the last four centuries on the subtle pleasures of the pipe.

ISBN-10: 1500441406
ISBN-13: 978-1500441401

Pipe Smoker's Notebook

This 60 page ruled notebook has a quote about pipe smoking on each page from some of the greatest pipe smoking thinkers of the past.

ISBN-10: 153041797X
ISBN-13: 978-1530417971

Order now from Amazon.com

Are you proud to be a pipe smoker?

If so, visit Pipe Gifts!

The Pipe Gifts online store is packed with items for the proud pipe smoker, including:

- T-shirts
- Mugs
- Cards
- Buttons/Badges
- Cufflinks
- Caps

Visit us today at
www.zazzle.co.uk/pipegifts

Lightning Source UK Ltd.
Milton Keynes UK
UKHW021830130119
335509UK00019B/354/P